W9-DDM-725

COLOR
& YOU

Discover how the right colors can make you look your best,
enhance your wardrobe, your image,
and everything you do!

by
CLARE REVELLI

PUBLISHED BY POCKET BOOKS NEW YORK

Permission to quote from *The Elements of Color* and *The Art of Color* by Johannes Itten, Van Nostrand Reinhold Co.

For additional information, please refer to page 47 or address:

REVELLI
1850 Union Street
San Francisco, CA 94123

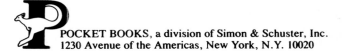

POCKET BOOKS, a division of Simon & Schuster, Inc.
1230 Avenue of the Americas, New York, N.Y. 10020

Copyright © 1982 by Clare Revelli

Illustrations by Paula Denman

All rights reserved, including the right to reproduce
this book or portions thereof in any form whatsoever.
For information address Pocket Books, 1230 Avenue
of the Americas, New York, N.Y. 10020

ISBN: 0-671-47274-7

First Pocket Books printing September, 1985

10 9 8 7 6 5 4 3 2

POCKET and colophon are registered trademarks
of Simon & Schuster, Inc.

Printed in the U.S.A.

Introduction

Discovering your best colors is easy and enjoyable with the concept of *Seasonal Color Theory* which is based upon nature and the predominant colors of the four seasons: Spring, Summer, Autumn and Winter. Each season is marked by its own dramatic set of colors or "seasonal palettes." Spring, with its bright shades of yellows and greens bursts forth with freshness and clarity; Summer unfolds in the pastel tones of blues and pinks creating a feeling of softness throughout; Autumn emerges with rich warm earthen hues of golds and browns; and Winter shines in the primary colors and the sharp contrasts of black and white. In Seasonal Color Theory, the colors of one season become you most. The harmonious and complimentary colors of that season give you a *Personal Palette*, an array of colors to use in selecting a wardrobe, that will be automatically color coordinated and always make you look great.

Dressing in your best colors, your *Personal Palette*, will have a great impact on your life. With a conscious awareness of the colors that make you look most attractive, you can affect the way people respond to you. Imagine going into your wardrobe and pulling out any combination of pieces that are automatically color coordinated and make you look terrific. Learning to select a wardrobe containing the colors that enhance your own natural coloring, those you have inherited – the color of your skin, the color of your hair, the color of your eyes, is the essence of Seasonal Color Theory. No two people are identical. Everyone has a unique skin, hair and eye color combination. There are certain colors which will compliment these traits that nature has given you. Other colors will clash, make you look less attractive and detract from your natural good looks. When you have finished reading this guide, you will know the colors you look best in, the colors which suit your specific physical characteristics. Dressing in your ideal colors will give you a sense of well-being, a sense of confidence that will carry over into your social and business relationships.

Color & You will identify your seasonal type and guide you in the use of your *Personal Palette*.

The best way to use this guide is to turn now to the charts on pages 38–41. Refer to the shaded boxes which list all of the possible characteristics for each season. Compare your own skin, hair, and eye colors, matching them with the box that best resembles your own characteristics. This will tell you the correct season that belongs to you. Remember that the *skin* is the most important characteristic to consider.

Awareness of Color

Though we may not always be consciously aware of color, it constantly surrounds us and influences us significantly. Daily we find ourselves having to make choices that involve color. Should I buy that sweater in navy blue or in pale yellow? Will I look better in this dark green suit or that light tan one? To make good color decisions that subsequently determine the way you look, the way you feel and how other people respond, you need to develop a thorough awareness of your Personal Palette, those colors which compliment both you and one another. Seasonal Color Theory gives a very easy method of determining exactly what these colors are.

Color, like the notes of a scale, has its own special harmonic qualities and intricate relationships. Often these aspects are not even apparent to the human eye. Color is the sensation you receive when the retina of the eye is stimulated by light waves of varying lengths. These reflecting light waves produce the primary (red, yellow, blue) and secondary (orange, green and violet) colors of the spectrum. The following terms are used to describe the differences among the more than 45,000 named and identified colors.

Hue: One of the pure bright colors on the color wheel which contains the primary, secondary, and tertiary colors.

Tint: when white is added to a color

Shade: when black is added to a color

Value: the lightness or darkness of a color determined by tinting or shading

Intensity: the brightness or dullness of a color. Mixing colors produces dullness. An unmixed hue is fully intense, vivid, bright and pure.

Two major classifications exist: "cool" and "warm." The difference in distinguishing a cool color from a warm color is in the blue or red which is added to a color. A touch of red in a color warms it, while adding a little blue cools it. In Seasonal Color Theory this principle is used for selecting each season's colors. Summers and Winters should wear only cool colors, whereas Springs and Autumns should only wear the warm colors. Examining the color palettes in this book will assist you in making the distinction between these two classifications. By comparing colors whenever possible, the perception of coolness or warmness in certain colors will become more apparent.

Johannes Itten, a great modern color theorist and a member of the Bauhaus School, taught that individual color preferences are highly intuitive. He believed we prefer those colors most in harmony with our spiritual expressions. In his definitive work, *The Elements of Color*, Itten reminds us that "the deepest and truest secrets of color effect are... invisible even to the eye and are beheld by the heart alone."

Most likely, the way you select your wardrobe colors is from your intuitive feelings. But sometimes decisions are made from impulsive attractions. You may be persuaded to choose pieces for your wardrobe which do not coordinate with one another or highlight your natural coloring. Trust your intuition. Most of the time, the same colors you are intuitively attracted to are the very ones you look best in.

Try this exercise to help you understand better the

notion of intuitive or subjective color preference. Look carefully at the color palettes in this book. Now, select the palette which contains the colors you feel most drawn to. You will find that the palette you have selected probably will be the one that corresponds to your seasonal type.

Here is another visual test to understand your personal colors. Gather several fabric samples of different colors such as bath towels, fabric remnants, table linens or items of clothing. Choose a location which has natural daylight and place a mirror in front of you. Hold each color up to your face, carefully noting which shades bring out a natural glow in your skin. Be certain to look at your face, not the color. Keep your attention focused on which shades best enhance your skin tone. It will be easy to select the flattering from the unflattering colors. Organize the fabric samples into two separate groups. Now refer to the palette you have been intuitively attracted to. You will be surprised to see how the most flattering group coincides with the colors in this palette. Have a friend or two join you during this session. They can assist in confirming your intuitions and learn Seasonal Color Theory at the same time.

Having done these exercises, you are starting to become consciously aware of the colors that attract you. Seasonal Color Theory, explained in the following section, combines knowledge, judgment and intuition to give you guidelines for developing a sense of color awareness and consciously managing the color in your life.

Seasonal Color Theory

It is easy to understand the concept of Seasonal Color Theory by dividing color into nature's four seasons: Spring, Summer, Autumn and Winter. The colors of your skin, hair and eyes provide the primary keys to a discovery of your seasonal type. For each season there is a corresponding palette of twenty colors. The twenty colors of each seasonal palette have been extensively researched and contain the best colors possible for each season. Special attention was given to proper shade and intensity as they relate to inherent characteristics of the skin, hair and eyes of each seasonal type. By wearing and experimenting with these twenty colors, you will quickly learn how to expand upon your palette colors even further. Personal Palettes act as a base group for each seasonal type and additional colors may be selected from tints or shades of the same basic hues. Within each Personal Palette the first five colors are neutrals. These colors are ideal for certain items of clothing such as coats, hats and accessory items like shoes, belts and bags. These neutral colors are also for someone who prefers less color in their clothes. Worn separately or mixed with other neutrals, these colors act as the foundation for each palette.

By wearing your Personal Palette colors, you will bring out the natural beauty that nature intended you to have. This enhancement will definitely affect your mood and have impact on those around you. It will provide a noticeable sense of confidence. Wearing your correct seasonal colors can also act as a visual vitamin. You will appear neither weak nor pale.

Color is strong magic. Color has power. It affects our opinions and relationships with others. During a first encounter with a person, we focus on the face, responding to the skin, hair and eyes. From the face, the eyes quickly scan the rest of the body. Whether we are consciously aware of it or not, the colors belonging to this new individual make an impression on us, even before we have exchanged a handshake or a greeting. If this person happens to be wearing correct Personal Palette colors, our subconscious forms a positive impression that says, "This person is in harmony." Wearing colors that are incorrect for one's seasonal type creates a negative subconscious response. Beyond clothing, color performs some role in almost everything we do. Surrounding ourselves with our best colors will create a pleasing environment, one that is aesthetically and physically attractive.

Understanding Seasonal Color Theory has advantages beyond those of image, personality and emotion. It is often difficult to make sound clothing purchases because of trends dictated to us by advertising campaigns and the fashion industry. Every fashion cycle brings with it much that is not designed for your particular seasonal type. Your closet may contain many outfits, perhaps bought impulsively. There may be too few that please you and fewer still that coordinate with the rest. The key to assembling an exciting, economical clothing collection is your twenty color Personal Palette.

Once you have discovered your seasonal type and Personal Palette and understand how to use it, you will plan purchases carefully. Most important, shopping for clothes that fit into your seasonal type is an economical idea. A color coordinated wardrobe lasts longer because it is interchangeable in many ways making for longer wear. If these purchases are made wisely and with careful attention to quality fabric as well as construction, they will be lifelong investments. Ever-changing fashion cycles will never influence your color choices as you will not have to compromise with what fashion designers dictate is "in."

To illustrate the idea of economical clothing purchases by using Seasonal Color Theory, imagine that you have discovered that you are a Winter. Having already familiarized yourself with your Personal Palette, you are ready to make some new clothing investments. While shopping, you have in mind the specific colors which best suit your needs. A Winter could enjoy lots of use from a coat that is either black, white or gray since these three colors are considered neutral in that season's palette. The purchase of a shirt, blouse or sweater is easier since your Personal Palette contains the most flattering colors for you. All others are quickly eliminated. Having your color direction defined saves time, money and mistakes.

No one can ever be a two-season person, or a person of all seasons. Johannes Itten states in *The Art of Color*, "Every woman should know what colors are becoming to her; these will always be her subjective colors and their complements." Modern color theorists argue that the same experience applies equally to men. Any person who is keenly aware of his or her physical being is more apt to enhance that natural beauty. By studying and practicing Seasonal Color Theory, the best qualities of your natural beauty and personality will become visible.

How To Determine Your Seasonal Type

Skin tone is the first and most important factor in determining your seasonal type. Skin contains a combination of three pigments which determine skin tone: melanin, which produces a brown tone; carotene, which shows up as yellow; and hemoglobin, which gives a red cast to the skin. Various combinations of these three pigments provide the skin with its own particular tone. You can tell whether your coloring is of a cool or warm type by observing the tone cast just underneath the skin's surface. A Winter or Summer seasonal type has skin that manifests a cool or blue undertone. A Spring or Autumn person has skin that shows a warm or golden undertone. Your skin tone is a unique quality that will not change during your lifetime. A suntan may deepen the tone of your skin and age may fade it somewhat, but you will never change from one season to another.

Your skin tone is the most important characteristic to consider in discovering your season. The second and third characteristics, hair and eye color, merely serve as a confirmation of whatever the skin tone has already indicated. To determine true skin color, carefully inspect the inner side of your wrists, disregarding the blue of the veins. Compare the color of this area with someone else's by holding a piece of white paper under each wrist. Does your skin show a blue or blue-pink undertone? If so, then you are most likely either a Winter or Summer type. If your skin shows a golden or golden-orange cast, you are either a Spring or an Autumn. Some people may find that their skin looks slightly sallow; this should not be mistaken as a Spring or Autumn's golden undertone. Any seasonal type may have sallow skin. This is a slight yellowish cast that may prevail all over or just in certain places, such as the arms and the face. Sallowness can also appear with age. It is important to look beyond this in considering your skin type. The white paper placed beneath your wrist will clearly define a blue or golden undertone.

Next, take a look at your face and study your skin tone carefully. Are there any particular traits which stand out in your skin? For example, capillaries can contribute to a ruddy complexion, causing the face to appear pink. This, like sallowness may be somewhat misleading. Look beyond the capillaries. Is there a rosiness to your cheeks? Do you have freckles, and if so, are they light golden brown or charcoal brown? Does your skin take on a clear translucent appearance? Jot down any noticeable skin traits which come to mind and keep them for further reference in determining your seasonal type. The charts on pages 38–41 will assist you in assigning any specific trait to its proper season.

The second most important step in determining your seasonal type is a candid examination of your hair. There is a simple trick to understanding your hair color as it pertains to Seasonal Color Theory. Take a moment to remember the color of your hair as it was when you were a child. It often provides the clue to confirming your particular season. Hair colors can vary greatly and have a tendency to change shades, with a gradual darkening trend as one ages. Your own natural hair color is usually the one to maintain, as it best compliments the skin and eyes in your seasonal look. Dyes can be used if they are selected with an eye toward the correct colors for your season. Now take a moment to scrutinize your hair as you have previously done with your skin. Do you have highlights, and if so, are they blonde or red in color? Have you grayed prematurely and is this a salt and pepper gray or a golden metallic gray? Is your hair a striking intense color or is it somewhat mixed and possibly a bit mousy? Again, note your findings and then refer to the charts in this book on hair color. Remember, even though your hair darkens naturally with age, your seasonal type will always stay the same.

Now that you have taken a good look at both the color of your skin and hair, you are ready to study your eyes. This will assist in confirming the conclusions already suggested by your skin and hair type. After studying your eyes in front of a mirror, try to note the one color which appears most predominantly. If your eyes are hazel brown with hints of gray, note which of these colors stands out the most. If they are of a chameleon nature (many colors), decide which color prevails most of the time. Does there appear to be a gray rim around the edge of the iris? Do you see small flecks of yellow or brown in your eyes? Do they tend to be more blue-gray or green rather than just a true blue? Record your findings and refer once again to the charts on eye color on pages 38–41. Remember that natural daylight will best assist you here.

When you have determined the color of your skin, hair, and eyes, you are ready to conclude that you are a Spring, Summer, Autumn, or Winter. Compare your findings for skin, hair, and eye color with the text and charts that follow for each specific season. The illustrations will act as an aid in showing typical traits from each of the various seasons. By matching your characteristics with those listed in the respective seasons, you will have easily confirmed your seasonal type and corresponding Personal Palette.

Classic Spring

Skin, Peach-Pink;
Hair, Golden Brown; Eyes, Topaz Golden Brown.

Spring

The Spring Person Is Naturally Full of Freshness and Vitality

Spring's skin has a golden undertone. Spring types have a skin that tends to be lighter than Autumn's with more visible color. Peach or fresh pink tints often prevail, giving a lively appearance to this skin tone. The Spring person may have very fine skin and is the most likely of the seasonal groups to blush easily. Light golden freckles are not unusual, though Spring's skin can be very clear and flawless. Check carefully to determine whether your skin is ivory, peach or light beige, a peach-pink or golden beige. Do you have a tendency to be rosy cheeked?

A Spring person probably has yellow blonde, golden blonde, blonde-red, auburn or golden brown hair. A strawberry redhead could also be a Spring. Highlights are usually of the 'golden red' shades. Some Springs will have golden gray hair.

Spring's eyes project brightness and clarity. They may be bright blue with turquoise, clear green, or clear blue, aqua, bluish-green or variations of light brown, from golden to topaz. Examine the following illustrations on Spring people. They will display the traits mentioned above.

The charts on page 38 summarize a Spring's characteristics and provide helpful information for the color schemes that should be used in clothing and accessories.

Spring

Skin, Golden Beige;
Hair, Golden Blonde; Eyes, Clear Green.

Spring

Skin, Peach-Beige;
Hair, Yellow-Blonde; Eyes, Aqua.

Spring Palette

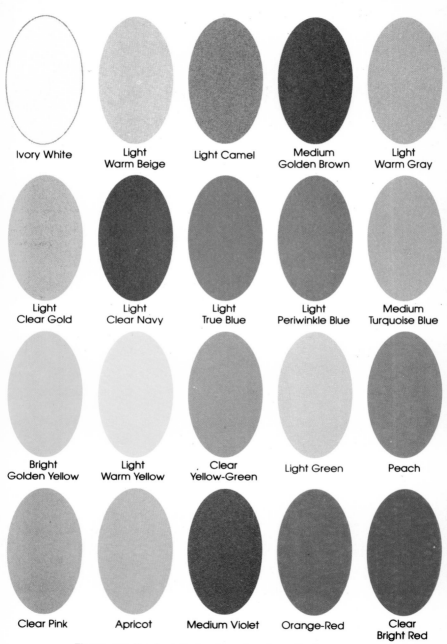

Ivory White	Light Warm Beige	Light Camel	Medium Golden Brown	Light Warm Gray
Light Clear Gold	Light Clear Navy	Light True Blue	Light Periwinkle Blue	Medium Turquoise Blue
Bright Golden Yellow	Light Warm Yellow	Clear Yellow-Green	Light Green	Peach
Clear Pink	Apricot	Medium Violet	Orange-Red	Clear Bright Red

These are the twenty basic colors for a Spring person.
Depending upon an individual's varying characteristics,
lightened tints or darkened shades of these colors may be added.

Spring

Because Spring's coloring is the most delicate of all seasons, choose colors that come alive. Look for clothing that is bright and clear, never faded or muted. Springs look their best in colors that contain yellow and should wear lots of it. The strongest palette colors should be worn by dark-skinned Springs, while those with lighter complexions should generally choose the lighter colors.

Do...
wear white with an ivory cast, an eggshell yellow.
choose only golden browns.
make certain to wear lighter grays with a yellow cast.
include lots of lighter navy blue in your wardrobe.
remember blue-greens and turquoise are fine for Springs.
wear lots of periwinkle blue, light blues, corals, apricots and peaches. All are excellent.

Do not...
wear pure white except far away from your face.
choose pastels as they are too weak and do not allow Spring's radiance to show through.
wear black unless it is confined to small prints.

Classic Summer

Skin, Pale Beige with a tinge of Pink;
Hair, Platinum Blonde; Eyes, Clear Blue.

Summer

Summer People
Have an Aura of Softness,
Simplicity and Peacefulness

Summers have a blue undertone to their skin and look their best wearing cool colors. A Summer type tends to have translucent skin with a tinge of pink in the face. By once again checking the skin color inside your wrist, you may easily confirm these criteria. If your skin is rosy colored, pink, light beige with a tinge of pink, or even beige and a bit on the pale side, then it is probable that you are a Summer type. If there are freckles, they will range from a medium to dark brown in color.

Check your hair to see if it matches Summer's description. Summer has ash blonde, smokey blonde or brown, dark taupe brown, brown with a slight reddish cast, bluish-gray or platinum blonde hair. A key: Summers will usually have golden blonde highlights in their hair as opposed to golden red highlights.

If you feel that you are a Summer, check to see whether your eye color supports the traits of this season. Summers have either blue, bluish-gray, greenish-blue, hazel, rose brown, soft gray, green or occasionally light aqua-colored eyes that change depending upon colors complementing the face. The iris will often have a gray rim around it or contain white flecks. Eyes of the chameleon nature are not uncommon. The Summer illustrations in this guide will confirm some of the characteristics listed here.

For a quick review and summary of Summer's traits, refer to the charts on page 39. Appropriate colors for a Summer's wardrobe and accessories are also listed.

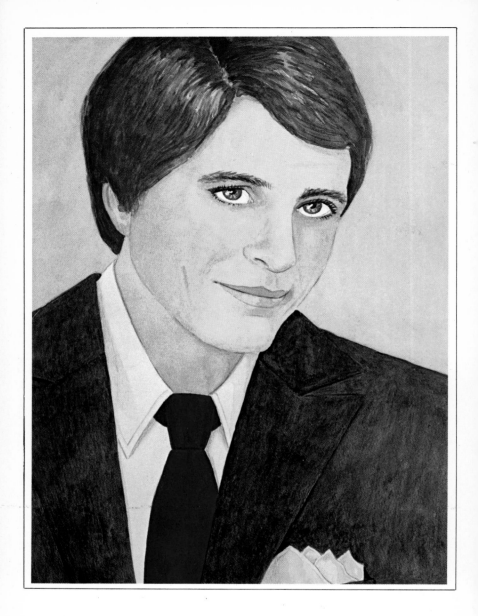

Summer

Skin, Light Beige;
Hair, Brown with a Taupe cast; Eyes, Soft Rose Brown.

Summer

Skin, Rosy Pink with Medium Brown freckles;
Hair, Smokey Brown; Eyes, Gray-Blue.

Summer Palette

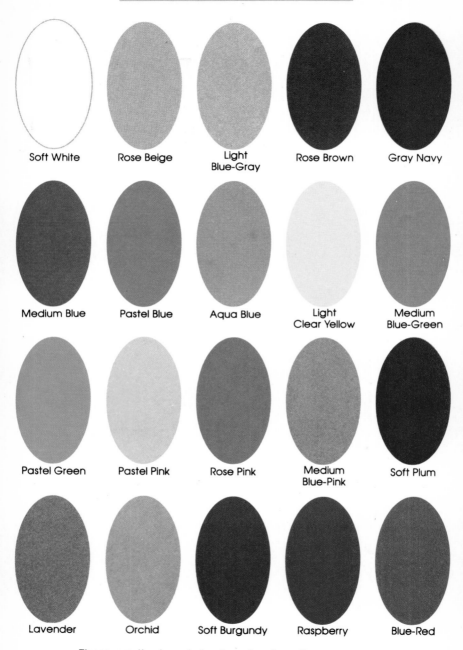

Soft White
Rose Beige
Light Blue-Gray
Rose Brown
Gray Navy

Medium Blue
Pastel Blue
Aqua Blue
Light Clear Yellow
Medium Blue-Green

Pastel Green
Pastel Pink
Rose Pink
Medium Blue-Pink
Soft Plum

Lavender
Orchid
Soft Burgundy
Raspberry
Blue-Red

These are the twenty basic colors for a Summer person.
Depending upon an individual's varying characteristics,
lightened tints or darkened shades of these colors may be added.

Summer

Summer's pale translucent look must not be over-powered by color. Any strong color will be overbearing. Pastels are Summer's best choice, especially those with a soft, bluish hue. When Summers wear the darker colors from their palette, they should complement them with something from the lighter shades. Remember sharp contrasts, such as black and yellow, are too severe. However, one wonderful combination for Summer is red, white, and blue.

Do...
choose only soft white.
stick with rosy beige and cocoa brown.
wear grays with a blue cast, light blue-gray or softened blue-gray charcoal.
include lots of blue; almost all light to medium shades are excellent.
remember any color with a bluish cast is your best bet if it is not too strong.

Do not...
wear much yellow unless it is very light, never golden.
pick any reds with orange in them.
choose pure black, white, gold, orange or any color with a yellow undertone.
wear black except as an accessory and never next to your face.

Classic Autumn

Skin, Coppery Beige;
Hair, Reddish Brown; Eyes, Yellow-Brown.

Autumn

Autumn People Are Especially Strong and Warm

An Autumn's skin tone will have a golden cast to it. Even if your face is the weathered sort, your skin will appear more orange than blue. Autumns can have skin that is ivory or peach colored. By the same token, they can be freckled redheads or black-haired and have copper-colored skin. In any case, whether the skin is white or copper, Autumn has an unmistakable golden undertone. Scrutinize your skin now. Is it either dark beige, beige (perhaps a bit sallow), peach, ivory or golden black? Frequently there are freckles that are golden blonde or light brown.

If you are an Autumn, your hair may be black, but will most likely be within the variety of warmer colors such as red, dark brown, light brown, reddish brown, yellow-gray or golden blonde with red highlights.

Autumn eyes are peacock blue, jade green, deep to pale greens, hazel, yellowish brown or light to dark brown. Flecks in the iris will be gold, brown, or citron. Compare the characteristics listed here with the following illustrations.

The Autumn chart on page 40 serves as a quick reference for your inherent characteristics. The color information on clothing and accessories will prove helpful in your purchases.

Autumn

Skin, Peach;
Hair, Golden Brown; Eyes, Peacock Blue with aqua tones.

Autumn

Skin, Ivory with Light Brown freckles;
Hair, Red (carrot top); Eyes, Jade Green.

Autumn Palette

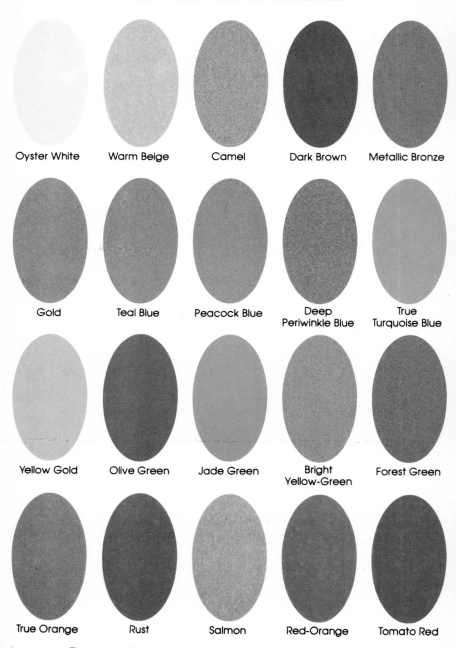

Oyster White | Warm Beige | Camel | Dark Brown | Metallic Bronze

Gold | Teal Blue | Peacock Blue | Deep Periwinkle Blue | True Turquoise Blue

Yellow Gold | Olive Green | Jade Green | Bright Yellow-Green | Forest Green

True Orange | Rust | Salmon | Red-Orange | Tomato Red

These are the twenty basic colors for an Autumn person.
Depending upon an individual's varying characteristics,
lightened tints or darkened shades of these colors may be added.

Autumn

Of all the seasonal types, Autumns have the largest selection of colors. Because they look so good in earth tones, they find the largest selection in stores since designers choose more of these colors. Autumns can safely wear muted or clear and vivid colors. Extra options are available to fairer skinned Autumns since they can wear pastel and lighter versions of the stronger colors in their palette. The key to looking great as an Autumn is remembering the colors of fall foliage. Gold tones are Autumn's best colors.

Do...
wear any shade of orange.

choose dark brown - excellent always.

substitute melon for pink.

select greens with a yellow cast in light or dark shades.

remember that Autumn's white must be beige-white, an oyster or eggshell.

think about dye or rinse if your hair looks drab or yellow-gray.

mix two or three variations of the same hue; for example, true orange might be worn with rust or salmon or a more neutral shade from the palette.

Do not...
wear navy blue, black, pink, gray, or any red with blue in it.

choose yellow unless it is distinctly yellow-gold.

Classic Winter

Skin, Milk White;
Hair, Black (with a blue cast); Eyes, Dark Blue.

Winter

Winter Types
Are Made Of
Clarity, Drama and Elegance

If your seasonal category is Winter, you will notice that your skin tone is either black with a blue undertone, beige, olive, rosy beige, white, white with a slight rose or red tone or milk white. If there are freckles, they will be dark brown or charcoal. Winters seldom have rosy cheeks. Blacks, Orientals and most olive-skinned persons are Winters.

If your skin tone belongs to any of the above categories, check your hair color for further Winter type characteristics. Winter's hair color will be either salt and pepper, silvery, white-blonde, white, black with a bluish cast, or medium to dark brown with possible red highlights.

If both your skin and hair fit into one of the above descriptions, then your eyes will most likely follow suit in telling you whether or not you are a Winter type. If you are a Winter, you have either black-brown, red-brown, blue-gray, medium blue with a gray rim around the iris, deep blue, grayish green, green with a possible gray rim, or hazel colored eyes. The Winter illustrations will confirm some of the above characteristics.

Refer to the Winter chart on page 41 for a quick summary of the typical Winter characteristics. Suggestions for wardrobe planning are also included.

Winter

Skin, Medium Olive;
Hair, Black; Eyes, Dark Brown.

Winter

Skin, Black with Blue undertone;
Hair, Black; Eyes, Dark Brown.

Winter Palette

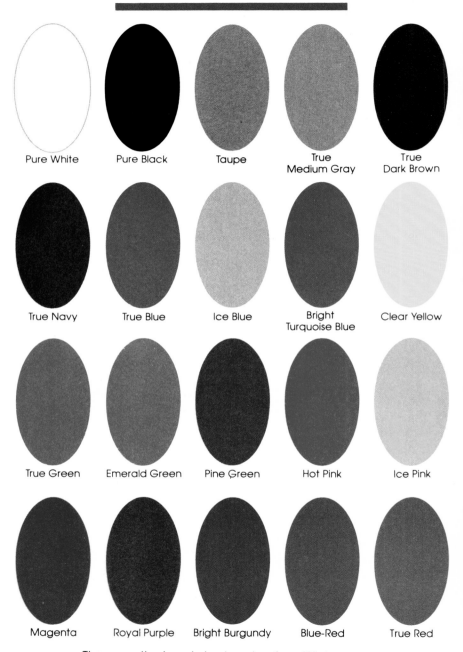

Pure White   Pure Black   Taupe   True Medium Gray   True Dark Brown

True Navy   True Blue   Ice Blue   Bright Turquoise Blue   Clear Yellow

True Green   Emerald Green   Pine Green   Hot Pink   Ice Pink

Magenta   Royal Purple   Bright Burgundy   Blue-Red   True Red

These are the twenty basic colors for a Winter person.
Depending upon an individual's varying characteristics,
lightened tints or darkened shades of these colors may be added.

Winter

There are more Winters than any other seasonal type because of their dominant genetic structure; the recessive genes of the other three seasons cannot compete.

Winters should always choose clear, vivid and sharply contrasting colors. Softened, faded, muted or pastels are poor, because they tend to give Winter a pale or weak look. Winters should wear only two colors at a time, never more than three. The best combination is black and white. Winter is the only season that can successfully wear those colors alone.

Do...

wear lots of primary colors.

limit tints (colors washed with white) to gray or pink.

stay away from any but rich, true browns. Men should be careful selecting suits and jackets.

wear only pure, bright burgundy.

distinguish between icy and light colors. Icy colors in Winter's palette are fine.

include lots of navy blue in your wardrobe; it's excellent for all Winters.

remember to select only taupe, a gray-beige, from the many beiges available to you.

Do not...

ever wear oranges, gold, yellow-gold or rust tones.

wear any whites which have yellow in them.

choose faded or muted colors.

Spring

Skin

Golden Beige Undertone
Ivory, Peach
Peach-Pink, Peach-Beige
Light Beige, Golden Beige
Freckles:
Light Golden Brown

Hair

Yellow-Blonde
Golden Blonde
Blonde-Red
Strawberry Blonde/
 Redhead,
Auburn, Golden Brown
Golden Gray

Eyes

Clear/Bright Blue
Aqua
Blue with Turquoise
Bluish-Green
Clear Green
Light Brown
Golden to Topaz Brown

Hair Dyes

*Warm, golden or
reddish tones.*
Yellow-Blonde
Golden Blonde
Golden Brown
Red Brown
Strawberry
Red or Golden Henna
Avoid partial Gray,
 cover completely
Avoid frosting

Make-Up

Foundation:
Yellow-toned Beige
 (for light skin)
Gold-toned Beige
 (for dark skin)
Ivory, Peach
 (light to dark shades)

Blusher:
Peaches
Corals
Peach-Pinks

Eye Shadow:
Soft Apricot
Green, Aqua
Soft Brown

Lipsticks:
Coral, Peach
Warm Peach-Pink
Clear Light Red

Spring Men

Suits - Slacks - Jackets
Light Beige
Light Camel
Medium Golden Brown
Light Warm Gray
Light Clear Navy
True Blue Denim

Dress Shirts
Ivory
Light Beige
Light Blue
Light Warm Yellow
Pastel Green
Apricot

*Sport Shirts - Sweaters -
Ties - Ascots*
Refer to Personal Palette
 Colors

Shoes - Belts
Brown, Tan,
Black

Accessories

Shoes - Belts - Bags
Ivory, Camel
Tan, Navy
Medium Brown

Jewelry:
Delicate and light of
 design; Filigree

Metals:
Gold tones
Brass, Copper
Enamels – in Palette Colo
 brushed or shiny

Stones:
Pearls (cream shade)
Coral
Jade (apple green)
Ivory
Moonstone
Emerald
Topaz

Eyeglasses:
Golden Brown, Ivory
Neutral or Palette Colors
Metals (see above)
Harmonize with individua
 hair color

These are your ideal colo
For additional selections re
to your Personal Palette.

Summer

CHARACTERISTICS

Skin

Blue Undertone
Light Beige
(with a tinge of Pink)
Light Beige
(no color, slightly pale)
Rosy Pink
(translucent)
Freckles: Medium to Dark
Brown

Hair

Platinum Blonde
Ash Blonde
Smokey Blonde
Smokey Brown
(with reddish cast)
Dark Brown
(with taupe cast)
Blue-Gray

Eyes

Blue (Clear, Sky Blue, Aqua,
may have white flecks)
Gray-Blue
(may be chameleon)
Soft Pale Gray
Green
(may have white flecks)
Hazel
(with Blue/Brown,
or Green/Brown)
Rose or Soft Brown

Hair Dyes

Cool, ashen tones
Ash Blonde
Ash Brunette
Gray: natural or highlight
with a rinse for highlighting
Frosting or light streaking
Avoid any red tones

Make-Up

Foundation:
Rose toned Beige
Pink Beige
Rachel Base

Blusher:
Light Pink
Rose
Blue-Pink
Light Plum

Eye Shadow:
Blue-Gray
Rose/Mauve
Soft Brown
Soft Gray

Lipsticks:
Pale Pink
Softened Plum
Light Burgundy
Blue-Pink

Summer Men

Suits - Slacks - Jackets
Rose Beige
Light Blue-Gray
Rose Brown
Gray Navy
Light Blue Denim
Soft Burgundy

Dress Shirts
Soft White
Rose Beige
Light Blue-Gray
Pastel Blue
Pastel Pink
Light Yellow
Aqua Blue

*Sport Shirts - Sweaters -
Ties - Ascots*
Refer to Personal Palette
Colors

Shoes - Belts
Light Brown
Navy Blue
Dark Burgundy

Accessories

Shoes - Belts - Bags
Light Brown
Gray
Bone-Rose
Off-White
Navy

Jewelry:
Fragile, finely etched;
lightweight and
uncomplicated design

Metals:
Silver, Rose Gold
Pewter, Platinum
White Gold
(brushed or shiny)

Stones:
Rose or Blue Pearls
Rose Ivory
Cameo
Amethyst
Aquamarine
Rose Quartz
Opal
Garnet

Eyeglasses:
Rose, Mauve, Gray or Blue
Neutral or Palette Colors
Metals (see above)
Harmonize with individual
hair color

These are your ideal colors.
For additional selections refer
to your Personal Palette.

Autumn

CHARACTERISTICS

Skin

Golden Beige Undertone
  Pure Ivory
  Peach
  Golden Beige
  Coppery Beige
  Golden Black
  Freckles: Golden Blonde
  or Light Brown

Hair

  Red (carrot-top)
  Reddish Brown
  Golden Brown
  Golden Blonde
  Charcoal Black
  Bronze or Metallic
  Gray

Eyes

  Dark Brown
  Golden Brown
  Yellow-Brown
  Hazel
    (Brownish-Green
    with Gold)
  Deep to Pale Green
    (Gold, Brown
    or Citron flecks)
  Jade Green
  Peacock Blue
    (with aqua tones)

Hair Dyes

Warm, Red highlights,
Auburn, Golden Brown tones
  Golden Blonde
  Golden Brown
  Red Brown
  Red, Strawberry
  Red Henna
  Gray: best to cover gray
    unless overall and a
    pleasing natural shade
  Avoid frosting

Make-Up

Foundation:
  Yellow-toned Beige
    (for light skin)
  Copper-toned Beige
    (for dark skin)
  Ivory
  Light to Dark Peaches

Blusher:
  Oranges (all)
  Gold tones
  Tawny Peaches

Eye Shadow:
  Green (Olive)
  Brown, Copper
  Soft Turquoise

Lipsticks:
  Peach, Coral
  Orange-Red
  Brownish-Red

Autumn Men

Suits - Slacks - Jackets
  Warm Beige
  Camel
  Brown (all shades)
  Bronze
  Olive green

Dress Shirts
  Oyster White
  Light Warm Beige
  Camel
  Brown
  Salmon
  Light Turquoise Blue

Sport Shirts - Sweaters -
Ties - Ascots
  Refer to Personal Palette
  Colors

Shoes - Belts
  Brown
  Tan
  Black

Accessories

Shoes - Belts - Bags
  Brown (dark and light)
  Tan
  Bone (Camel)
  Gold tones
  Olive

Jewelry:
  Strong, bold designs,
    wooden pieces,
    tortoise shell

Metals:
  Antique Gold
  Bronze
  Copper
    (brushed or shiny)

Stones:
  Cream colored pearls
  Carnelian
  Leaf-green Jade
  Turquoise
  Cinnabar
  Agate
  Amber (dark)
  Smokey Quartz

Eyeglasses:
  Red-Brown or Tortoise Shell
  Neutral or Palette Colors
  Metals (see above)
  Harmonize with individual
    hair color

These are your ideal color
For additional selections refer
to your Personal Palette.

CHARACTERISTICS

Skin

Blue Undertone
Milk White (colorless)
White
  (with slight Red/Rose
  undertone)
Beige
  (with slight sallowness)
Rosy Beige
Olive
  (light to dark)
Black
Freckles: Dark Brown,
  Charcoal

Hair

Black
  (with blue cast)
Brown
  (medium to dark,
  possible red highlights)
Blonde (White)
Salt and Pepper
Silver-Gray
White (snow)

Eyes

Black, Dark Brown
Brown
  (with a reddish cast)
Hazel
  (with varying shades of
  Gray, Green, Blue)
Green (with white flecks)
Gray (with Blue or Green
  combination)
Medium Blue
  (with white flecks)
Dark Blue

Hair Dyes

Cool, ashen tones
 Ash Brown, Ash Blonde
 Blue-Black
 Natural or Black Henna
 Gray: natural or highlighted
  with a rinse
 Avoid frosting, bleaching or
  streaking
 Avoid all red tones

Make-Up

Foundation:
  Rose toned Beiges
    (medium to dark)
  Pink Beige
  Honey Beige
  Rachel Beige

Blusher:
  Rosy Red, Blue-Pink
  Burgundy, Plum

Eye Shadow:
  Lt. Gray/Silver
  Lt. Plum/Mauve
  Blue-Gray
  Ash Green/Blues

Lipsticks:
  True Red, Blue-Red
  Burgundy, Plum

Winter Men

Suits - Slacks - Jackets
  Pure Black
  Taupe
  Dark True Brown
  Dark Denim Blue
  True Navy
  Gray (light to dark)

Dress Shirts
  Pure White
  Light Taupe
  Clear Yellow
  Light True Blue
  Light True Gray
  Light True Green

*Sport Shirts - Sweaters -
Ties - Ascots*
  Refer to Personal Palette
  Colors

Shoes - Belts
  Black
  Navy Blue
  Dark Brown
  Dark Gray

Accessories

Shoes - Belts - Bags
  Black (also Patent)
  Navy Blue
  Dark Brown
  Dark Gray
  White, Bone (Taupe)

Jewelry:
  Understated and simple
  design. Enamels in primary
  colors.

Metals:
  Platinum, Silver
  Chrome
  White Gold
    (brushed or shiny)

Stones:
  Pearls (Black or White)
  White Ivory
  Diamonds/Zircon
  Emeralds, Crystal
  Sapphire, Lapis Lazuli
  Rubies

Eyeglasses:
  Blue, Burgundy, Gray-Blue
    or Black
  Neutral or Palette Colors
  Metals (see above)
  Harmonize with individual
    hair color

These are your ideal colors.
For additional selections refer
to your Personal Palette.

41

Commonly Asked Questions

What are the differences between the "Cool" and the "Warm" seasons?

The difference between the "cool" seasons, Winters and Summers, is primarily in their skin tone. Summers usually have more of a visible pink in their complexion with a blue undertone in their skin. Though Winters share the same blue undertone, they tend to have more olive or beige skin as opposed to the fair or translucent skins of Summers. Springs and Autumns are "warm" skin types. Both have a golden undertone in their skin and share the same fair complexion. Springs tend to have rosy cheeks and will flush easily. Autumn's cheeks are usually pale.

How do you decide which season you are if your eye or hair color does not correspond with your skin tone in matching one of the charts?

Your *skin* tone should always be the deciding factor in determining your season. You could be misled in choosing the correct season if your hair has been either dyed or bleached by the sun. Be certain to use your natural hair color to support your findings on the skin tone you have noted. If you wear tinted contact lenses, remove them prior to determining your eye color.

What colors can all seasons wear well?

All seasons have about four *compromise* colors that they can wear: either a soft white without any hint of yellow, coral, light aqua or deep periwinkle blue.

Can a person be more than one seasonal type?

You cannot be more than one seasonal type, even though you might have a few characteristics that commonly belong to a different season. There are some theories that are based on a percentage of seasonal mixture when determining your personal colors. The theory as stated in this book dispels all doubt and confusion...your Personal Palette will help to simplify life, not clutter it with unnecessary options.

What is a "Classic" season?

A person who has physical characteristics that are typical for his or her season (i.e., a Winter who has black hair, dark brown eyes and olive skin) might be called a *classic*. Refer to the first sketch at the beginning of each season for examples of the classic seasonal types. The second and third illustrations display slight variations of a classic within the same season.

Does one's season change with age or with a suntan?

No. Although age may fade your inherited skin tone and a suntan may deepen it, your seasonal type will remain the same throughout your life.

Should you wear black if you are a season other than a Winter?

Black is normally too harsh a shade for any season to wear except for Winters. It can be worn by other seasons if it is kept away from the face and arms, such as with skirts, pants, belts, etc.

How do I select prints and patterns using Seasonal Color Theory?

Look for backgrounds and predominant colors from your Personal Palette. Small prints and accent colors from other palettes are acceptable as long as your overall attire is from your own.

Are family members usually all of the same season?

Often. However, there can be many differences among family members depending upon which genes are inherited.

Color and Feelings

From the moment we wake up, we are bombarded by the sensation of color. Color can have a very conscious effect on us but most of the time its influence is one of a subtle subconscious nature. The advertising world has long understood the importance of color and has used color to influence buying and to make products more appealing. Color can sell by calling attention to the product as well as imparting and defining information. Certain colors such as yellow and red are used more frequently because they have a more conspicuous attraction to the eye. These are "hot" colors, so to speak. They create attention almost immediately. In creative cooking, not only is the taste of a meal stressed but also its color. There is a strong correlation between the visual and olfactory senses. Meals that are well balanced colorwise are more appealing to the appetite and seem to taste better.

Chemists study color as it concerns pigments, dyes, and color fastness. Physicists explore color as it relates to the phenomena of light. Physiologists examine the relationships between eye and brain functioning by the way that they are influenced by color. Psychologists study the effect of color and how it influences behavior. All of these professions deal with color in a very specific way.

Indeed, there has been an incredible advancement in the world of color. Astounding technological development has brought color into our lives more than ever before. Not long ago, there were no color movies. Watching a film in color creates very different reactions than seeing it in black and white. Color can create messages, establish atmosphere, and influence feelings.

The four seasons of the year present another analogy of the impact color has on our feelings. The colors of a gray cloudy sky are misty and muted. The same can be said about one's general mood during gloomy weather. Spring, with the arrival of fresh flowers and bright colors, infects everyone with "Spring fever." Summer might evoke shades of soft pastels and blue tones, conveying a sense of peacefulness and tranquility. And Autumn brings with it all the earthen tones such as golds, browns, and moss greens – feelings of richness and warmth. The starkness of Winter's black and white contrast connotes a sense of drama and clarity.

Throughout history, symbolic meanings have been given to colors. These have come from the images and feelings different colors evoke.

RED signifies heart, birth, beginning violent change, energy, strong emotions, determination, courage, prominence, heat, divine love and charity, aristocracy, revolution, and joy.

YELLOW indicates faith, constancy, wisdom, glory, brightness, intellect, sensation, communication, speed, cheerfulness and logic.

BLUE symbolizes spirit, heaven, prayer, royalty, contentment, tranquility, love of good works and a serene conscience.

GREEN is symbolic of life and love, abundance, happiness, faith, and youth.

VIOLET is used to symbolize royalty, temperance, stateliness, dignity, richness and power.

ORANGE gives us the feeling of glory, radiant energy,

sunshine, vitality, illumination, fantasy, warmth, wit and humor.

Conscious awareness of color and discovering the colors that make you glow will give added dimension to your life. Color is a vital part of living. When used as a creative force, everything is brighter.

Quick Review Steps for Discovering Your Season

1. Stand in a place where plenty of natural light is available.

2. Hold the innermost side of your wrist over a piece of plain white paper. This will allow you to determine whether your skin has a blue or golden tone. If there is a blue tone, you are either a Winter or a Summer. A golden cast means that you are an Autumn or a Spring.

3. Next, standing in front of a mirror in natural daylight, drape yourself with fabric in the colors that belong to the two seasons you chose in Step #2 – either a Winter/Summer or a Spring/Autumn. Keep your attention fixed on which shades enhance your skin tones best. These colors will help you to identify which season you belong to. Be certain to look at your face, *not* the color. Try to have a friend work with you here if possible.

4. Confirm your discovery by checking your eye and hair coloring with the charts in this book.

MORE FROM *Revelli*

• *Revelli* 's "Four Seasons" Clothing Catalogues

My season is:

Spring ☐ *Summer* ☐ *Autumn* ☐ *Winter* ☐

☐ Please send me information about obtaining fabric swatches of my Personal Palette.

☐ I am unsure of my specific season. Please send information about the Revelli color analysis questionnaire and photo program.

☐ Please include me on the COLOR AND YOU mailing list for all *Revelli* clothing catalogues, special events, and seminars.

Name _____

Address _____

City _____ State _____ Zip _____

Home phone: _____ Business: _____

Mail to:

Revelli
Color and You
1850 Union Street, Suite 377
San Francisco, California   94123

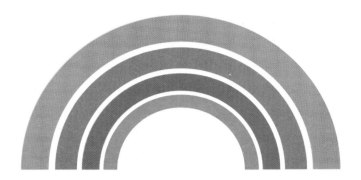

Clare Revelli has spent most of her life in the world of fashion and design. After studying at New York's Fashion Institute of Technology, she designed for several of the city's top fashion manufacturers. Clare returned to her native San Francisco Bay Area to design for a large knitwear firm and establish her own schools of clothing design. A popular speaker on fashion subjects with emphasis on color, she has served on the faculties of colleges in New York and California for the past ten years. She discovered seasonal color theory which was developed by Johannes Itten in the early 1930s and applied it to wardrobe planning that uses one's best colors or personal palette. Today, Clare heads her own design and consulting firm which specializes in the concept of Seasonal Color. Revelli's clients include JP Stevens, Clairol, Renaissance Eyewear, Celanese Fibers, Accessory Street and Sears.

Clare's seasonal products include cosmetics, eyewear, sunglasses, jewelry, accessories and clothing. Each item is labeled by its respective season: Spring, Summer, Autumn, Winter.

Discover, with Clare, the colors and clothes that will always make you look and feel your best.